I0475000

Now Pick Me!

A Practical Guide for being picked for the job ***You*** want

ISBN: 1453704329
ISBN-13: 9781453704325

Now Pick Me!

A Practical Guide for being picked for the job ***You*** want

Martin Fisher

CONTENTS

ACKNOWLEDGEMENTS

IT DOES NOT TAKE LONG to write the number of words required to fill the pages of a book, it does however take time and patience to write and edit a book so that it flows and achieves the goals it was written for. I easily wrote a lot of words for this book, but it has to be said that without the encouragement and feedback from a couple of people who helped me edit the copy, a real book would not have emerged. In this regard I would like to acknowledge the work of Stephanie Mitchell who did an edit of a very early rough draft of the book, and particularly Jill Jukes who invested many editing hours on many drafts, as well as helping to shape the many training programs we have run together.

For the graphics of this book and the accompanying website, I would like to thank Brent Parr at Optio Publishing.

And most importantly, I am so lucky to have an understanding family, who encourage such endeavors as this – to my wife Susan, who did the final read through and edit, and daughters Alex, Tori and Ella… Love you!

Martin.

INTRODUCTION

Why this book?

HAVE YOU EVER COME AWAY from an interview and felt that your performance did not quite measure up to how you had envisioned it before you went into the interview? You felt you didn't do yourself justice, or that the interviewer just didn't ask the right questions? And that was the one shot at the job you wanted!`

When we are looking for a new position it always feels as though there are too few suitable roles available and that there are many other qualified candidates going for the same job. With all these suitable candidates out there you would think a company should easily find exactly the right person for them. But it is not easy, and with fewer resources there is increasing pressure on hiring managers to just pick someone quickly so that they can get back to their own real job.

This book is written for people who are looking for their right job, a job that is a good "fit", a job that matches their skills and strengths and allows them to be successful and happy.

This book will go a long way to helping you get the job you want by helping you identify how you should positively represent yourself; helping you stand out from the crowd in an interview and ultimately get the employer to *pick you!*

The title, "Now Pick Me!" represents how you will feel after you have read this book... absolutely ready!

The characters on the cover of this book are called *darumas.* Originating from Japan, these characters are purchased with two white circles where the eyes should be. When you set yourself a goal you colour one eye in. Now put the one-eyed daruma were it can watch you. Daruma looks incomplete as he stares at you with his one eye. Daruma is reminding you that you have work to do to complete your project or achieve your goal. In your case, perhaps the one eyed daruma is reminding you that your goal is to get the job you want, and the work you have to do to get ready to achieve this goal is to read and actively participate in this book.

Once you have achieved your goal you are able to fill in the other eye of your daruma completing his gaze.

Daruma is complete... friendly with two eyes, compared to making you feel uneasy with one.

At the end of this book you will be able to fill in the second eye of your own personal daruma. You will be more confident going into your next interview because you have achieved your set goal of optimal job interview preparation, and you will be prepared to be the one picked for that job.

How the book developed

For many years, I have been involved in sales and marketing. Over that time, I have developed a "feel" for the concept called "positioning". It goes by many academic names and descriptions such as; "unique selling benefit" or "crystallized product promise", but in this book, I only refer to it by "positioning" and will attempt to make the concept real and practical to you. You will learn basic guidelines and processes for positioning and I will try to illustrate the concept with a number of personal stories about product launches, my interview experiences and projects I have led in the past. After working through this book you will feel comfortable using this concept for yourself, about yourself.

I have seen success when I followed these guidelines and failures when I tried to take short cuts – so my advice is to not take short cuts!

Over the years I have found that focusing on positioning changes outcomes and leads to success. I felt so strongly about the subject I developed a seminar that I present to anyone who will listen: colleagues, staff, other departments, partner companies and even customers.

I reached a point where I even discussed the concept and the presentation with a friend who worked in a career transition / out-placement company. Together we pondered whether positioning could be adapted for people looking for a job. Could we use the same guidelines and processes I used for a product to help someone find their own positioning, allowing them to stand out in an interview. I started presenting my ideas to classes at the out-placement firm, and over time I have continued to adapt the seminar based on audience feedback.

I have done this presentation for people from all kinds of industries, specialties and levels of responsibility and everyone has said they found my presentations to be very useful not just in their job search, but also in feeling proud of what they have already achieved in their careers.

This feedback encouraged me to go one step further to share my knowledge and expertise. My presentations combined with an article I wrote for the out-placement company's internal newsletter, were the springboard for this book.

The book is not necessarily unique in presenting this idea; however, I set out to write it as a practical tool for anyone to use in achieving their employment goals.

I encourage you to write in this book, highlight key points, fold pages and draw in it. The more you put into the process, the more productive and fruitful your personal journey and eventual outcome will be.

Chapter I

A PLOT FIT FOR REALITY TV

MARK BURNETT IS LIKELY A MAN whose work you either love or loathe. He has developed a number of hit TV series. In fact, he has arguably created a whole genre of TV. He was the producer of *Survivor*, the first mega-popular reality show. He has to be admired making *Survivor* a must-watch program and then following that up with other programs such as: *The Apprentice, The Restaurant, The Casino, Rock Star, Combat Missions* and *Pirate Master*. He has the ability to create situations in which a group of people (competitors) are put into an elimination-based, winner-takes-all situation. In these situations, the viewer can see how people react and interact under pressure, how they bond and work together, how they compete and, most importantly, how elimination decisions are made. Rarely do we see a majority decision from the audience or critics on who the winner will ultimately be… it would be too boring for the audience if you could predict the winner from the start. One of the keys to the show is that we get to see all the quirks of the human character under pressure – how different people come to different conclusions, and act differently even when they all receive similar input.

Hell's Kitchen, The Apprentice and the British Armed Forces!

Hell's Kitchen, and The Apprentice, have been very successful TV shows, commanding huge audiences and high-priced commercial advertising spots. The programs may appear trivial to some, simply a way to stroke the egos of their star performers and humiliate a number of contestants on an international stage in the name of entertainment, but at their core may be the right way for a person to find out if they like a particular job, and for the hiring manager to find the right employee. In these situations the "hiring manager" can see exactly how a candidate thinks and reacts in a near-real life scenario.

Personal Story: When I was just out of university I wanted to become an officer in the British Armed Forces. How do you think the British Army chooses the right people to be its leaders? Funnily enough, it was not just through a couple of one-hour interviews! As well as interviews with officers of all ranks, candidates are put through a series of challenging tests. Many of these are very practical, designed to identify candidate strengths and weaknesses. Tests include: leading and being part of a team navigating through obstacle courses, writing essays on strategy, and testing a candidates communication skills through participation in a number of group discussions on various topics.

Who knew that *Hells Kitchen, The Apprentice* and the British Armed Forces would have so much in common – a practical approach to the hiring process!

What if we created a new, two-episode reality TV show on interviewing where we turn on its head the logic of "how to best do hiring". We would create artificial pressure and allowing for quirks of human nature to take over?

First, we need a catchy title for the show....

Let's use "Now Pick Me!" as the working title. I'm sure you will come up with a better one as we go along.

How about placing a judge in a studio set in a cheerless office. The walls are bare, except for a couple of matching landscapes and a framed corporate vision document. The middle of the room has a round teak table, drink coasters and two or three black leather chairs around it. One of these chairs is obviously the seat of power, with a black binder and silver pen on the table in front of it. This is the judge's chair.

Now let's bring in 15 contestants, who, one after the other, come into the room to meet the judge for an hour each. This will take place over three business days. In that hour, the judge has to identify just *two or three* of the contestants who could potentially work for the company and who will go on to complete in the final round for the prize of *the job* - with a cool company car and a significant compensation package.

The judge is then allowed to re-interview the final contestants for another hour in the cheerless office. And then the Judge must choose one winner to get the job.

But the program has one more twist. After six months of working together, the judge must review the "winner's" work with the company. If the "winner" passes this review, there is a permanent job waiting for them. If the "winner" does not meet expectations, the job vanishes, and the hiring judge starts the process all over again!

The interesting part about this concept is that at this final step, if the judge says, "No, you were not the right choice", then the contestant is let go and no one wins. If the judge says, "Yes, you were the right choice," there are two possibilities. The judge may have said "yes" merely to avoid admitting he or she made the wrong decision six months ago! If everyone else in the company has concluded the winner was the wrong choice, then, again, no one wins. But if everyone in the company agrees that the judge made the right decision and the winner is a good hire, then everyone wins.

Confused? How do you like your chances in this kind of game?

In fact, as I am sure you realize, this *is* the reality in most job interview situations.

Reality in most cases

Unfortunately, perhaps due to a perceived lack of time or money to invest in the hiring process, the level of effort put into finding the right person *is* usually two or three hour-long interviews, with maybe some psychological testing for higher paying positions. We live in a job market where the hiring process generally looks like our *Now Pick Me!* reality show.

This leaves too much guesswork about whether a person is really the right fit for a particular job or company. There is very little chance of really finding out what a person is good at especially if, in the eyes of the interviewer, all of the candidates tend to act the same way and say very similar things in an attempt to impress! Too often this whole process relies on the interviewer's questioning skills in being able to tease out real differences between candidates in a short period of time.

On top of this, in an interview, there is usually a 10-minute general chit chat to calm everyone down at the beginning and 10 to 15 minutes at the end for any candidate questions. That really leaves just 35 to 40 minutes of questions and answers to find out whether the particular candidate is the best person for the job, and therefore to make the interviewer look like a hero for finding the best candidate.

Personal Experience: A number of years ago I interviewed a couple of young, newly qualified MBA graduates. The challenge I faced in this situation was that after I interviewed the second candidate, I had to check to make sure I had not inadvertently interviewed the same person twice. It seemed as if the candidate had left my office, put on a wig and tried to increase their chances of getting the job by being interviewed again. The candidates were too similar for me to *pick* between them. In the short period of time they had to talk about themselves, they focused on their MBA education rather than telling me how they had *uniquely applied* what they had learned, and why this would be particularly useful to my company and me.

I did not offer either of them the job.

Your challenge

Given this reality, what can you do to give yourself the best chance of being the winner and being picked for the job?

CHAPTER TAKEAWAYS:

- The current system used in most companies to find a new employee is not ideal.
- However, that's how the hiring process generally works.
- You must figure out how to make full use of the relatively short time opportunity you have in an interview to show how you can uniquely add value to the hiring company, if you want to be the one *picked* for that job.

Next Step

In the next chapter we will consider some of the dynamics that are going on in a job interview, in particular: what might the interviewer be looking for in an ideal candidate and why might this be the case? You will even get to role-play being the interviewer!

NOTES

Chapter 2

RE-FRAMING:

LOOKING AT YOU FROM THE OTHER SIDE OF THE DESK

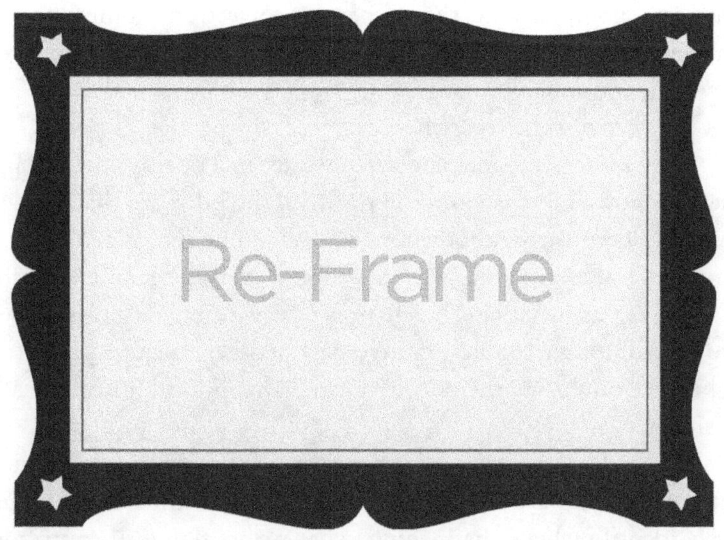

IF YOU HAVE EVER BEEN into a framing store to have a piece of art or a photo framed, you will already know that when you put different frames around a picture you see the picture slightly differently. Using different styles and colors of frames can bring out different colors in the art.

Such is life. Everyone has a frame through which they view the world. Think about your frame as a window frame or the frame of a pair of glasses. The frame can dictate how you see life around you and the people in it. Your frame has been developed over your lifetime, influenced by your parents' views and prejudices, your own feelings around experiences you have had and your education. Your particular frame means that when you see something happen you immediately jump to a certain conclusion about what must be happening... different people react differently to any situation because they see the situation unfold through their own individual frame. Think about how two people can look at the stock market at the same time, in completely different ways, one *bullish* and one *bearish.* One sees gloom around the corner, a "correction" coming to the financials to turn the tide of stock growth; the other sees opportunity with continued growth.

This can also be true when we meet new people.

If we meet someone new when we are in a positive mood, and the person we meet is similarly positive, the odds are that we will generally be positive about how we feel about that person. Conversely, if we are in a negative mood and everything and anything is irritating us, what are the chances that we are going to see even the friendliest and most positive new acquaintance in a positive light? We might see them as irritatingly happy and unrealistically positive!

We need to be able to *Re-Frame,* to look at ourselves, others and the situation we are in, in many different ways, in order to objectively identify what is happening, what we are doing to contribute to the situation and how we should react.

Reframing in your job search.

It is critical in an interview to really understand what frame the interviewer is looking at you through in order for you to really understand how you can make the most of your opportunity.

Have you ever thought about what it must be like to be on the other side of the desk conducting the interview with you for this job? It looks easy. You just sit there and ask questions from the sheet of paper on your clip board; then you just put a tick by the names of the ones that answer the questions correctly; then, you interview the people with the correct answers again and pick the one you like.

But is it really like that?

Let's change our frame and think like the hiring manager to learn more about how the company goes about finding the right person for their vacant position.

Be the interviewer.

Put yourself in the shoes of the interviewer. Identify what is likely really important to you, as the hiring manager. What would you be thinking? What might you be feeling? What pressure is having this vacancy putting on you? What strengths, competencies and skills are you really looking for?

Right now, in this *frame of mind,* fill out *Worksheet A* from the perspective of your next interviewer. You are the hiring manager. Think about *your* company and the role *you* are hiring for; think about how *your* company is performing and what impact this might have on the type of candidate you are really looking for. Later in the book, we will look at how you can find out some of these things, so do not worry if you cannot complete all of the worksheet right now. You can always come back and continually improve it!

Worksheet A

Role play – You are the interviewer

a) Who am I?

Name: ....

Company: ....

I report to: ....

b) Person I am hiring

New hire reports to whom? ....

Job title of position I am looking to hire: ....

I want the person in this job to do: ....

....

....

How does this position fit in the organization?

....

....

(Diagram)

With whom will this person interact most? ....

c) My Overall Objective as Hiring Manager

Write down in a few words what you are really trying to accomplish:

....

....

....

....

Reviewing your role-play answers from *Worksheet A*

I think you would agree that the questions in section (b) probably feel very general, and perhaps a little vague. However, knowing the answers will be critical for you to know as you go into your interview.

How would an interview go if you wrote different answers to the (b) questions?

Hopefully, in section (c), the last part of the questionnaire, you put things like:

To find someone who;

- has fresh ideas to change the role,
- can sort out the problems I have had with this position in the past,
- is an inspirational leader who can motivate this team,
- can take over from me when I get promoted/retire,
- can introduce processes to get us organized so that we can grow,
- continues to do the steady job the last person did, or,
- will be happy to stay in this position for just a few years before moving up in the company.

How would you react differently in an interview if you knew the answer to (c)?

There are many different objectives the hiring manager might have, but underlying all of these objectives is probably something like:

"The new hire will be accepted by everyone, especially my boss, my peers, and the rest of my team, as the best person for the job."

"Everyone sees I have made a great hire!"

Reality check: Everyone really *does* want to find the best person for the position! Honest! Even if sometimes they aren't really exactly sure how to achieve it.

What am I specifically looking for from my new employee?

Hiring managers must be prepared. They must know exactly what they want the new a hire to do in the job and what strengths the person must demonstrate in the job in order to succeed.

What is your ideal job? Take a few moments and become the hiring manager for that position. On *Worksheet B,* write down some of the things you might be looking for from the ideal candidate.

I recommend you photocopy this and all other worksheets, and I recommend using pencil as you will undoubtedly want to add, change and erase things as you go through the rest of the book and revisit the worksheets as you learn more.

Worksheet B instructions

In the far left column, "Looking for", write down a list of words describing what you would like to see from the person you are hiring. No jargon, be specific about what you want and be as clear, basic and honest as possible.

The next column is "Level demonstrated." In as few words as possible, state what level of expertise you want to your ideal candidate to demonstrate for the words in the left column.

In the column marked "Admission ticket?" put a star if you think this item is a "show stopper," i.e., if this strength is not demonstrated, then you will not hire this person, no matter how much you like them.

Finally prioritize the list in order of importance and place their priority number in the "Priority level" column. If you have lots of items pick the top five and use a one to five scale with five as the most important.

Example:

Looking for	Level demonstrated	Admission ticket?	Priority level
Doing lots of projects at the same time	Needs to talk about an example where they successfully dealt with a number of high priority tasks, with different teams, at the same time	✓	2
Done it before	Needs to have worked in this industry and done a similar role before	✓	1
Comfortable communicating in writing	Has written effective internal newsletters (asked to bring an example in, or asked to write one prior to the interview)		3

Reminder... You will come back to this page again and again, so I really recommend the use of a pencil.

If you have more than 10 items / rows you may not really be considering what the most important attributes are that you are looking for from the successful candidate.

Before prioritizing try to balance them all and cut back on the ones that are two general or do not stand out as really the most important factors in the hiring process.

Worksheet B

What am I looking for from my new employee?

Looking for	Level Demonstrated	Admission Ticket?	Priority Level

Personal Story: A story on the importance of viewing situations from a different frame. For career development purposes I took a negotiation course. There are many books and courses about all aspects of negotiating and I recommend you take advantage of at least one of them. My most important learning was that the best negotiations occur when there is a *win-win* outcome, i.e. both sides in the negotiation feel, at the end of the day, that they have both achieved what they needed to achieve to call the negotiation a success. To be happy with the outcome of the negotiation therefore you have to know what result you would be happy with from the negotiation <u>before</u> you start. This ranges from "what would you love to get", to "what is the least you would accept to be happy". It is also therefore important, early on in the negotiation, to find out what the other party feels they need to achieve from the negotiation for them to be happy. Often two negotiators find that they are actually looking for different benefits from an agreement … therefore it is possible for both sides to find a solution that makes them both happy. Bottom line: the more you know about the other side, i.e. through what frame they are viewing the negotiation, the better able you are to get to a *win-win* result.

How does the hiring manager identify you as the perfect person for the job?

Unfortunately, not all hiring managers are trained as well as they might be to conduct good interviews; many only interview once or twice a year.

No matter what the skill level of the interviewer, you have to make a good impression. You may be faced with an inexperienced or unprepared interviewer who provides no real structure in their hour with you and just hopes they will uncover what they need. Or, you may be interviewed by someone who has had extensive interview training, for example in a technique like *behavioral event interviewing*. In this type of interview, the overriding assumption is that the best predictor of *future* behavior (i.e. how will an individual react in a particular situation in the future) is to identify *past* behavior in similar situations. Before the interview, the interviewer identifies an ideal candidate profile (similar to your *Worksheet B*) consisting of skills, such as "key boarding" or "programming", and past behaviors such as "commitment to do what is required to meet deadlines" or "innovativeness". They then ask questions to find a candidate with these things, demonstrated by past behaviours. A trained interviewer will ask questions requiring you to give specific examples from your past proving your competency in these skills and / or experiences.

When this is done right, behavioural event interviewing is a great interviewing technique. It moves beyond basic answers, such as; "yes, I can key board", "yes, I can speak in public", "yes, I know about computers", etc. to "let me tell you about a time when I met a seemingly impossible deadline."

Your *team* experiences and accomplishments

The focus of interviews should be on what you have done, e.g. *what did you organize, plan, initiate* or *follow-up*? When you are answering questions about team activities, focus on what *you* accomplished within the team and the difference it made to the outcome of the team's activities... not just on what your team as a whole accomplished. If you were part of a team, the interviewer is really looking specifically at what you did as *part* of that team to achieve results. How did you *specifically* contribute to the team's success? For example, did you lead a particular part of the project? Did you find a way to do something not done before by a team as part of the process? Did you contact the customers when this would not normally be part of your regular job duties?

Personal Story: For many, this focus on *you* rather than *the team* feels a little strange. As an interviewer, I sometimes feel like I am "pulling teeth" to get many candidates to tell me what *they* actually did on a project team. For some time now, many companies have worked the concept of team into their credo and culture... in these companies you may even be personally measured based only on team results. So, thinking about what *you* did as an individual can feel awkward. Resist the temptation to commend the team and say how lucky you were to be part of that team, and how you wouldn't have been able to achieve your goal without all the other team members. Instead, focus and explain how the team worked, what value you added to the team as a member and how you enabled the team to work together to be successful.

What strength did you add to the team that helped it achieve its goals?

What *you* did is exactly what the interviewer wants to know.

What you added to that team might be just the thing they are looking for on their team.

Chapter Takeaways:

- The job is never just how it reads in the ad.
- Put yourself in the employer's shoes and imagine how it looks through their "frame".
- What are they really looking for from the new hire in this role?

Next Step

In the next chapter we will begin to review the core concept of marketing and the focus of this book - "Positioning". You will learn about some common brands and how they have become successful through focus and positioning. We will consider how we think about these brands and what it means to our general purchasing habits.

Chapter Acknowledgement: I would like to recognize Gareth Morgan, Distinguished Research Professor, Organizational Behaviour, for his teaching on re-framing at the Schulich School of Business. His lectures and insights helped re-frame my ideas for this chapter of the book.

Chapter 3

MARKETING 101

How did I get so wrapped up in this topic to the point that I have written a book on the subject?

For all my adult life, I have been in sales – selling products, ideas and people. Come to think of it I even sold myself as a kid to my parents: how good I had been so I could receive a treat, and how I deserved to stay up late to watch the end of a sporting event.

As someone involved in sales and marketing I've tried to unravel the whole sales process. Now I am adapting the selling of products to the process of being successful in interviews.

A trip to the supermarket.

Personal Story: When I was single I can't honestly say that I went to supermarkets very frequently. My idea of a meal was take-out, delivery, a restaurant or a convenience store. I lived in a downtown condo after all. When I got married, I discovered a whole new world, the phenomenon of grocery shopping at your local supermarket.

Now I had to decide what products we needed and which brands I should choose from the thousands on display.

Think about standing in front of a typical shelf in a supermarket for the first time of, say, toothpaste. Have you ever thought about what goes through your mind when faced with supermarket shelves piled high with different types of toothpaste? Probably not, read on and I'll have you seeing toothpaste differently!

When faced with a huge choice of brands of toothpaste, do you immediately reach for one specific brand without considering alternatives? Or, do you identify your favorite brand and then scan the rest of the products to see if there might be a cheaper one available, or one that better meets your specific needs? And if there is one cheaper available, for example, do you negotiate with yourself and rationalize whether the price difference between the two is close enough to justify you buying the first one you picked up?

Before we move on let's make sure we are clear about some of the terms I am using here as they will be important when we begin to look at ourselves as a Brand.

Product Category: A group of intrinsically similar items or services that we buy or use. Examples of product categories would include bottled water, pasta sauce, batteries, washing machines, computers, etc. Service categories would include; accounting, dog walking, dry-cleaners, etc.

Brands: The specific names of products that have, in some way, been *differentiated* from other products in the same product category. Examples of brands would include: *Coca-Cola, Perrier, Kit-Kat, Prego, Apple,* and *Duracell.*

Differentiation: What a company does with its product or service to make it a brand, standing apart from its competition. This may be achieved through; design, name, image, unique features, color, etc. *Generics* or *no-name* products are usually the most basic, non-differentiated products (without any "bells or whistles") and usually compete only on being the lowest price.

Have some fun and fill out *Worksheet C* to see if this is clear. I've given you a couple of answers to get you going.

Worksheet C

Products and Brands

Product Category	Two Brands
Cola	Coca-Cola and Pepsi-Cola
Sports cars	Lamborghini and
Breakfast cereal	
	Primo and Prego
	Rolex and Patek Philippe
Car rental agencies	
Headache pills	
	Mars Bar and Snickers
Supermarkets	
	Sean Penn and Kate Winslet

Choosing product A or B?

This whole process is explained in its simplest form in the book "*Positioning: the battle for your mind*", by Jack Trout and Al Ries. I first read the book in 1993 and it has been my sales and marketing guide ever since. I only scrape the surface of the concept here, and I highly recommend you invest in their book, which is an easy read and as relevant today as it ever was.

Trout and Ries offer a great visual to keep in mind when you think about the *positioning* concept. They describe our brain as having a "ladder" for each product category we may buy, and each product or service brand belongs on a certain rung of that ladder in our mind.

Let's look at an example to explain this idea. What happens when we stand in front of all those tubes of toothpaste in the supermarket? Our brain immediately goes to a ladder in our mind for the product category *toothpaste*, and we immediately think to reach for the brand on top of that ladder. This brand of the product (toothpaste) is the one we might commonly say is "top of mind"; it is the product we are *most likely* to buy. We may reconsider at the time of purchase, and eventually buy the brand on the second or third rung of the ladder, but we are less likely to move out of our comfort zone with a product lower on the ladder without significant effort and thought. This is true especially with product categories we purchase frequently. We know which brand will make us *comfortable* and *happy* with our purchase. As Trout and Ries also explain, ladders for products we buy relatively frequently (such as, perhaps, chocolate bars – for me anyway!) may have many brand rungs, while things we buy less frequently (like washing machines), tend to be shorter with fewer brand rungs on them. Test out whether this is clear – *Worksheet D* has product category ladders, followed by spaces (ladder rungs) for you to fill in the brands. Choose some product categories of your own and see how many brands you can name. How about: soap, TV manufacturers, pizza companies, chocolate bars, shampoo or breakfast cereals.

Worksheet D

How many rungs on the ladder?

	Toothpaste	Soft Drinks	Hotel Chains	(You pick a category)
1				
2				
3				
4				
5				
6				
7				
8				

When thinking about a common product category ladder you will find that your mind will be able to deal relatively well with up to seven different brands (i.e. you will have very fast recall of the first two to three brands, a slower recall of brands four through seven and then a real time lag before you identify an eighth brand, if at all!). Check this out on your *Worksheet D.* How many brands did you name for each product category ladder you attempted, and how easy was it to get to that number? If you did not do the worksheet, do it now, do it as quickly as possible and see how your brain does.

Look again at which brands you have written, and, more specifically, at the order in which you have put them. There is a very good chance you have put the category leader at the top of each list, and the second most successful product in second place, and the third in third place. What about that fourth, fifth, sixth and seventh products you thought of? There's a good chance that these brands are not doing so well in the market, and are fighting for the scraps of market share left by the top two or three.

The key thing to remember is that the product at the top of the ladder is the brand the customer is most likely to buy.

What do you do as a marketing manager if you decide to launch a new brand in a specific category, but there are already lots of well-known brands on the top rungs of the ladder, such the soft drinks market with *Coke* and *Pepsi*? Do you just have to spend more to become the top brand?

Many companies, with many brands, have tried to get to the top of the ladder by just spending more money on advertising and promotion than the market leaders… and failed. This is not the way to build a successful brand where an established product category ladder already exists.

The way to build a successful brand in this situation is to establish your own, new and unique ladder with your brand at the top of it! The product differenciation you select however must also relevant to your audience. It must be compelling and be a reason to choose your new ladder over another.

The classic case study

Take the soft drink brand, *7-Up*. When *7-Up* set out to establish itself nationwide, it was not just as a soft drink, doing so would have invited direct competition with the mighty and powerful *Coca-Cola* and *Pepsi*. Instead, the brand team for *7-Up* created their own ladder with its own perceived value-added benefit for the customer: it was the alternate drink to *Coke* or *Pepsi* and became known through advertising as the "Un-Cola"! *7-Up* was for that time when you craved soft drink, but not a cola. In one short sentence, they renamed the ladder with *Coca-Cola* and *Pepsi* on top of it as a "cola" ladder, and established a smaller, but significant ladder for themselves called the "un-cola" ladder. What if the *7-Up* team had just settled for a place on the already existing "soft drink" ladder? Where did *7-Up* come on your soft drink ladder? It was not likely higher than third at best. But *7-Up* would likely have been top if we had called that particular ladder the "un-cola" or "non-cola" soft drink ladder! The new ladder will likely never be as large as the cola ladder, but for a new entry into the market, being top of a small ladder is better and more sustainable than sixth or seventh on a larger ladder. Think about this as you see commercials on TV. Consider whether the brand being promoted is on a ladder with an established leader, or rather , attempting to create a new ladder for their brand. Many product categories have a number of ladders developed within them - through good brand differentiation. See if you can name a few on *Worksheet E.*

Worksheet E

Name a new ladder!

Original ladder	New ladder	Next new ladder
Hotel	Cheap no frills hotel	Suites with kitchens
Cola	Un-cola	
Shampoo		
		Groceries delivered to your door
	High grade gas	Unleaded
		DVD / Blu-ray
Sony Walkman		

Why is Positioning Important to You?

What is common between what we have so far talked about in this chapter and looking for a new job?

- There is a customer (hiring manager) who is looking to purchase (hire).
- There are likely a number of candidates for the hiring manager to choose from (competitors).
- There is only a limited amount of time in which the hiring manager must make a decision about each candidate (advertisement time).
- There is a product that has to make an impression and stand out from the crowd... YOU!

So, from what we have learned so far, how do you go about positioning yourself?

How would you describe yourself in an interview setting right now?

Are you a *non-differentiated, generic product*? If this is true, to the interviewer, you are no different than the other candidates and you are less likely to be chosen?

Or, are you a *promoted, differentiated brand* owning a specific, unique ladder in the interviewer's mind?

Chapter Takeaways:

- For *any* sales and marketing success your brand must be differentiated from its competitors.

Next Steps

Before we move on to the next steps in finding your own positioning, or, your ladder to own, let's review what is actually happening in an interview.

Chapter Reference: Positioning: The Battle for Your Mind. Al Ries and Jack Trout; copyright *2001 by The McGraw-Hill Companies, Inc. (first published 1980).*

NOTES

Chapter 4

INTERVIEW DYNAMICS

LET'S THINK FOR A MOMENT - interviews should *not* be a one way process!

Both you and the company are actually selling *each other*.

You are going in to *sell yourself* (your positioning) to the company, showing that you are an ideal candidate who can add the value they are looking for, and, if they want you, the company will be *selling themselves* (their positioning) to you, demonstrating why you should want to work for them. They will sell themselves as top of their ladder.

Good companies understand that every personal interaction is important. Even if they don't offer you this job, they should still be selling you their company. After all, at some point in the future you might be the perfect fit for another position in the company and they might come looking for you!

Going into your first interview, you are basically an *undifferentiated product.* Most candidates will likely have similar qualifications – screening of resumes does this. The interviewer learns the *brand name* of your particular *product* (your name). The interview should then quickly move to assessing why you might be different - how you might add value to their company. What are your unique abilities and do you have a track record to support your claims?

Both your resume and your interview must make your unique positioning VERY clear.

Remember, you want to differentiate yourself from the crowd of other candidates, and *own* the top rung of a ladder of your choice.

Deciding what this ladder should be is the most difficult thing to do in marketing. It is therefore the most important thing for you to do for your career.

Doing this will be the focus of the next part of this book!

Chapter Takeaways:

- The interview process should be two-way… there are specific attributes and skills the interviewer will be looking for from you, and there should be specific information they will be imparting to you about themselves.
- An interview is also an opportunity for you to find out what the company is really all about. Are you sold on the company at the end of the interview? If not, why?

Next Steps

The next two chapters will guide you on the research needed to create your own ladder and positioning with the hiring company.

NOTES

Chapter 5
YOUR "SELF" AUDIT

Defining your ladder

LET'S START BY DEFINING SOME potential ladders you can choose from.

Turn to *Worksheet F*. In the left-hand column, write down what you feel you are good at. At this point the exact wording is not important; it is just important that you start jotting down your *strengths* (what you do well). As we discussed earlier, it is not enough that you can list a series of strengths, but you must be able to demonstrate these strengths through stories about past accomplishments. Keep your descriptions short, sharp, and to the point. You can elaborate more and practice talking about your accomplishments later once you identify the strength you wish to highlight most in an interview. Also, remember that one story, depending on how it is told, may support a number of strengths.

Example for *Worksheet F*

My Strength is:	And I can support this with the following true success story (or stories):
Multi-tasking	Last year, I organized a charity fund raising event and the company's biggest-ever advertising campaign in the same week. Both were successful. The charity raised a record amount, and the campaign achieved a 20% increase in sales.

Note: The strengths and support statements do not have to be exclusively work-related. For example the strengths may be best exemplified by your outside work activities, such as hobbies or volunteer work.

Strengths – *Skills* and *Competencies*

Your strengths may be either skills or competencies.

The Strength Iceberg

Strengths in the form of *technical skills* can easily be demonstrated. Skills are tasks learned and repeated and potentially validated through some form of a certificate, license or diploma, or even a simple test (such as in keyboarding or use of a computer program).

Strengths in the form of *behavioral competencies,* however, are much more difficult to identify and measure e.g. *leadership, process innovation* or *ability to work well in a team.* Everyone has different competencies; it is a matter of defining each and identifying the level of ability you have in the competency.

Leadership levels example:

Level 1. "shows some ability to lead small teams on well defined projects", or

Level 2. "can lead large diverse teams through well defined projects", or

Level 3. "is experienced and capable company leader under pressure".

To truly claim a competency at an appropriate level, you must demonstrate it when under pressure or stress. During times of stress, people naturally rely on their core competencies to manage a situation.

The iceberg figure (shown) represents the ease of differentiating skills from competencies. Above the waterline the iceberg represents *skills*: easily identified and documented. Under the water line, the iceberg represents *competencies* which can only be uncovered by looking at past behavior, or possibly through role-playing scenarios.

In nature, most of an iceberg is below the water line. For successful interviewers, identifying your *core competencies* is not only difficult but critical as, like the iceberg, the *competencies* are the foundation on which you stand.

Find ways to facilitate the process of uncovering your *core competencies.* Arrive prepared to tell anecdotes describing these hidden strengths.

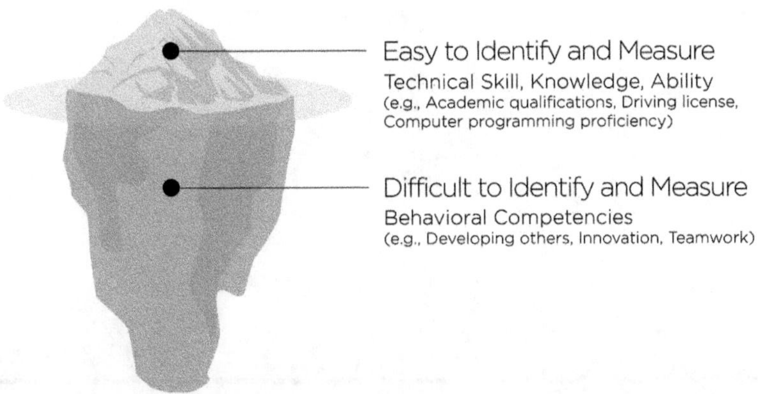

Appendix I provides you with some competencies that you can use to prompt your thinking. If you choose one from the list, make sure it is actually one of your supportable strengths!

Worksheet F

My Strengths – Skills and Competencies

A strength is:	Accomplishments to support my strengths:

One thing you should notice after completing *Worksheet F* is just how many strengths you have.

You can start on a second worksheet if you like.

Be proud of what you are good at!

If you are really having trouble identifying strengths, ask people who know you well, such as your friends, close colleagues and family to tell you what they think your strengths are. You may be pleasantly surprised at the number of strengths they believe you have.

Once you have finished *Worksheet F*, take your sheet to someone you trust for an honest opinion. This person could be a mentor or perhaps a former colleague or boss who knows you well. Ask them to look at the list and give you honest feedback on what you have written down. Ask them if they agree with the strengths, if you have missed anything or if there is a better example of how you have demonstrated any particular strength. Be gracious. Sometimes this feedback may be hard to take. Try not to become defensive. Remember this feedback is how they see you through <u>their</u> "frame" – this is basically your current positioning with them! You will benefit most from this exercise if you get, and accept, truly honest, constructive feedback.

Chapter Takeaways:

- You *do* have many strengths that you can support and be proud of.
- Some of your strengths will be in the form of *skills* that are easily demonstrated to an interviewer, and some will be in the form of *competencies* that you will demonstrate through the use of anecdotes and stories of your past behaviors.
- It is critical that you evaluate all your strengths with someone you trust to give you honest feedback.

Next Step

You have a collection of strengths for yourself. But this is only half of the story. Now let's move on to identify a little more about the company you are interviewing with. From this research we will then match up which of your strengths should be your positioning.

So what do you need to know about the company you are interviewing with? How do you find the information and how do you deal with conflicting information?

NOTES

Chapter 6

DOING YOUR HOMEWORK THE MARKET RESEARCH PLAN

REMEMBER, AS THE SAYING GOES, you only get one chance to make a great impression, and this is especially true when you go into an interview. If you aren't prepared, the job will slip out of your hands and there may be no second chance. Consider every interview a live "first night performance" for your own reality show! Once you have been chosen for an interview you begin the process of differentiating yourself from all the other candidates.

What you need to know before going into the interview

In the ideal situation, you know as much key information about the company as possible, for example:

- What is their key market?
- What are their key products? Who are their competitors? What is currently happening in their industry? What markets are they planning to enter?

- How does the company really work?
- Is there a new management team? Do they have expansion plans? Are they stock price driven?
- What is the company's positioning with partners and customers?
- Check it out! What is the reputation of the company, the hiring manager, the unit you may be joining?
- What is the real purpose of the job itself?

Ideally, you will know this information better than the other candidates, and perhaps even the company itself!

In order to really impress, you need to know within what context (or frame) the position will be viewed. For example, is the company an established, big-spending, brand-focused company with well-defined roles and responsibilities (bureaucracy, paperwork, standard operating procedures), or is it a young upstart company, questioning everything established, and that basically flies by the seat of its pants?

Would you approach these two kinds of companies in different ways?

Once you know the company's current situation, you need to establish where it wants to be in the future, what it needs to get there (or remain there) and what implications that may have on the demands of the vacancy you are interviewing for.

How do you find this company information?

Worksheet G is your guide to figuring out where you can find the information you need before you go to an interview. The internet is now a standard starting point for many, but do not take everything you find on the internet at face value. Like a good news reporter, try to get at least two sources to confirm each fact. Evaluate the information you gather; the internet, books, magazines, trade associations, and people are your key resources. Every source of information will be slightly different as each person or media will have their own frames of reference through which they view the company. Use these different views, and pull them all together to get a more accurate 3-dimensional view of the company.

People as a resource

This is a good time to test the *six degrees of separation* theory; that is, if the people you know are considered one degree from you, and the people they know are two degrees away from you, then everyone in the world is connected by no more than six degrees of separation. So the person who is looking for someone like you to fill a position perfect for you, is closer than you think... you just have to connect with them! With the advent of internet networking tools, such as *LinkedIn* (*www.LinkedIn.com*), testing and using this theory is getting easier.

Worksheet H gives you some guidance as you decide how to assemble all the company information once you have collected it.

Worksheet G

Where to find company information

Who / Where	Name / Address	Complete by (Date)	Completed? (Yes/No)
Current employees			
Past employees			
Customers			
Non-customers			
Competitors			
Partner companies			
Recruiters			
Annual report			
Sales data			
Financial / Business press			
Websites			
Industry			
Competitor			
Company's own site			
Blogs			

Worksheet H

What I now know!

Category	What I learned	Source
Culture What is it like to work there?		
People Are people happy? Is there much turnover?		
Development and training Do they usually promote from within?		
Position in industry What are the numbers?		
Growth Is it growing, stable, or declining in the market?		
Innovators Is it a leader or a follower?		
Current Issues Internal		
Current Issues External		
Role-related challenges?		

Be Aware

Again, remember that all of these sources of information, whether written or spoken, will have some sort of bias due to their different frames of reference. No one source will be *the* accurate source. For example, the current employees or the corporate websites may be just promoting the company line and not reflecting reality. The ex-employee may be disgruntled and have a personal axe to grind. The supplier or customer you talk to may have just had an exceptionally good or bad experience with the company and not reflect the company's larger reality of customer service. The take-home message is this: always collect multiple points of view (frames) of the company. The more frames you find the more accurate and clear your own view will be.

Consider talking about some of your findings in your interview. This shows that you are curious, interested and have cared enough to investigate the company beyond the normal level of general candidates. It also gives the company's representative the chance to talk about what is important to you about the company. Remember however not to break any formal or informal confidences under which people initially discussed the company with you.

Working backwards

Now that you have completed *Worksheet H* with your new knowledge, it's a good time to go back and review and amend *Worksheet A* and *Worksheet B*. Knowing what you now know about the company and its people (again put yourself in the shoes of the person interviewing you) would you take a different approach to the question of what the company is really looking for in a successful candidate?

Chapter Takeaways:

- You will get out of the interview only as much as you put into it.
- The more you know about the company, it's people and it's business the more confident you will be discussing how you are going to add value to their company.
- Look to multiple sources to gather your information, and combine them in order to get the most realistic view of the company.
- As you go along, you need to continually review and evaluate your earlier Worksheets.

Next Steps

You now know what your strengths are, and you have uncovered the situation of the hiring company in terms of its own market and how the company works. You have also reconsidered what the hiring company might really want from the job in question. In the next chapter you will now put worksheets F and H together to finalize your positioning. While there is much art to doing this, the following chapter will help you take an analytical approach to reach a final positioning.

Chapter 7

YOUR LADDER – *YOUR* POSITIONING

I AM SURE YOU WOULD agree that undervaluing yourself in an interview situation is definitely *not* something you want to do.

Why do we sometimes undervalue ourselves? Part of the challenge, I believe, is that we sometimes feel anyone can do what we can do well and, in some cases, we fear others will always be able to do it better than us. It may also be that we have been raised to not boast about ourselves, or feel that we should stand out from or seem better than others.

The best way to present yourself is with confidence. Know how you can help the company achieve its objectives. Identify therefore, which personal strengths should be the focus of your interview.

Positioning – Science vs. Art

This, for many, will be the most difficult part of this book. You may want this to be a pure science, where we just assign numbers to get the concrete "true" answer. That would be so simple. But, as in any marketing endeavor, we are dealing with human interactions, and human interactions are not simple!

The interview is very much an art, but as an interviewee you can still use some numbers and some analysis, to help direct your focus in the interview.

Remember, there are no *right* or *wrong* answers when it comes to positioning yourself. I can describe to you the positioning for the most successful product ever, and there still might have been an even better positioning for the product leading to more sales.

Now, don't get the wrong idea here – this is not an excuse to broaden you ladder description to find some wording that covers more than one strength. You must be as specific as possible in your ladder selection; otherwise you will be indistinguishable from all the other candidates. You must have one specific ladder that you are top of, that you *own*. Why? Any brand, and particularly your personal one, can not mean all things to all people. When you try to encompass everything in your positioning, you will end up with descriptions meaning nothing to anyone because you have taken away the one key point of differentiation.

Work with friends and mentors to identify the one ladder, the one key message that you can make your own. You should now see the value of the work you did in Chapter 5.

Rating and Ranking Your Strengths

How do you choose your ladder from your list of strengths? Here is a guide to help you to identify your options and likely positionings. Remember – there will always remain a certain element of *art to this process.*

Worksheets Ia and Ib

In the column marked "Strength" on Worksheet Ia, write down what you feel are your top eight strengths (skills and/or competencies). It is fine if you have less. Also make sure you list strengths you have identified the interviewer will be looking for from candidates.

Under "Level of Strength," rank each strength, with your strongest strength an "8" and the weakest of your strengths as a "I".

Under "Importance/Relevance," rank your strengths for importance, or relevance, in the mind of the interviewer. That is, based on your research, which of your strengths do you think the interviewer is looking for in the ideal candidate? Rank each of your strengths from "8", down to "I" as you did in "Level of Strength."

No cheating, no two strengths can have the same ranking!

On Worksheet Ib, plot your strength rating on the "*y*" axis. Plot your rating of each strengths importance/relevance to the company on the "*x*" axis.

The example below is a comparison of two strengths, "ability to juggle priorities" and "public speaking".

In this example, we have concluded from our research that "public speaking" is the higher priority of the two to the hiring company. You know that it is not a key strength for you and therefore it is unlikely you can own this ladder in the minds of the interviewer. As your "ability to juggle priorities" is very high (6 out of 8) you might therefore conclude that your positioning should be your "ability to juggle priorities". During the interview your job is to "sell" the interviewer why "ability to juggle priorities" is, in fact, the key strength they should be looking for; then demonstrate you have this particular strength to successfully secure the job! This is the art over the science.

Alternately, you may conclude you need to raise your "public speaking" strength through training or practice to the point where you can move the "public speaking" spot up into the "Sweet spot" range.

Strength	Level of Strength	Importance / Relevance
Ability to juggle priorities	7	6
Public speaking	3	8

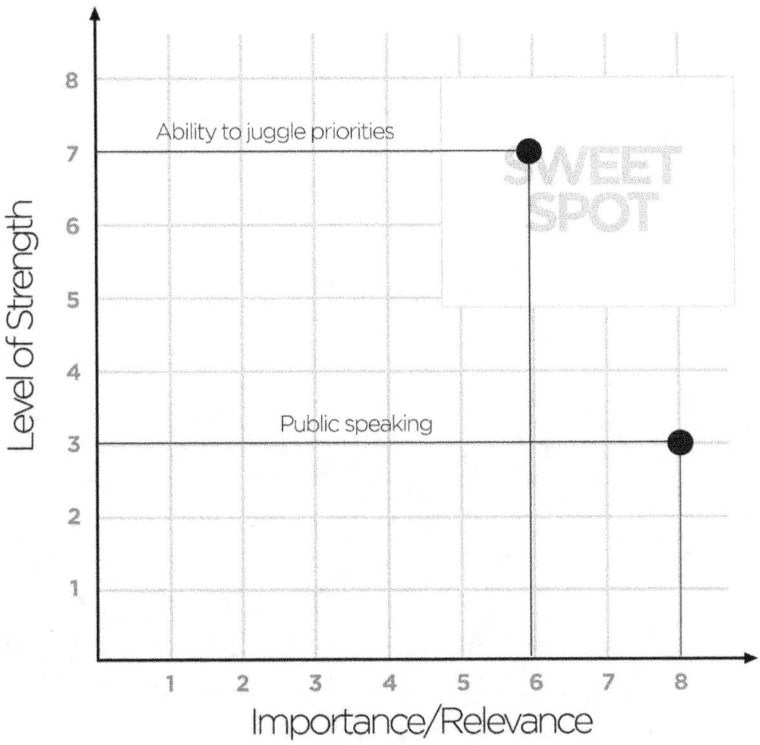

Worksheet Ia

What I now know!

	Strength	Level of Strength	Importance / Relevance
1			
2			
3			
4			
5			
6			
7			
8			

Ratings / Rankings
Level of Strength
8 = My highest rated strength 1 = My lowest rated strength

Importance / Relevance to organization
8 = The most important / relevant strength for this position
1 = The least important / relevant strength for this position

Worksheet Ib

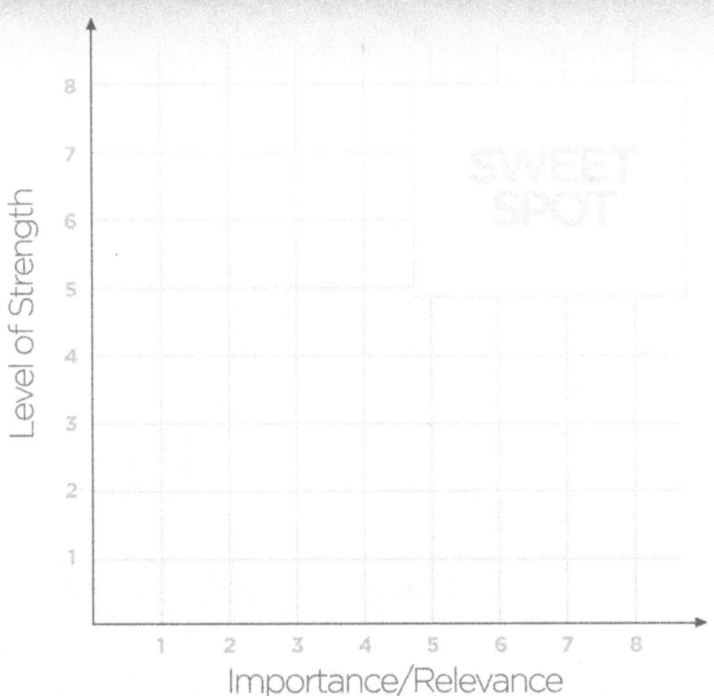

Analysis of Results

If this really were a pure science, what might you conclude? Based on the worksheet, you may suppose the best / most appropriate positioning is whatever strength is in the uppermost right corner of the sweet spot; this may well be the case.

a) Win-Win

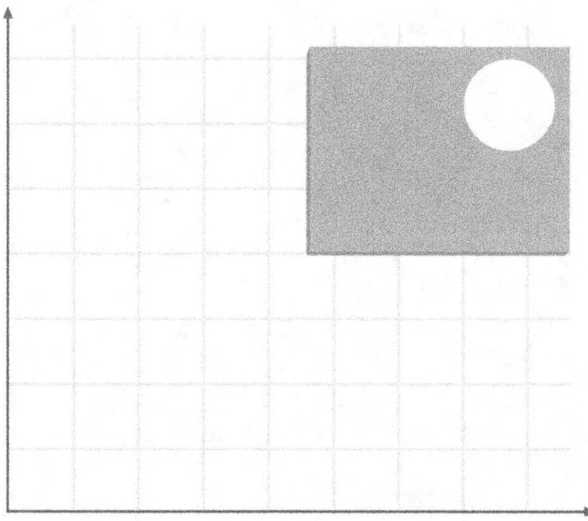

Here we have the perfect scenario, your top strength is the top strength the company is looking for to fill their vacancy. Now, you must communicate this strength, with appropriate stories to support it, in order to have the best shot at owning the ladder and getting a job offer!

b) Undervalued, Lower-Strength

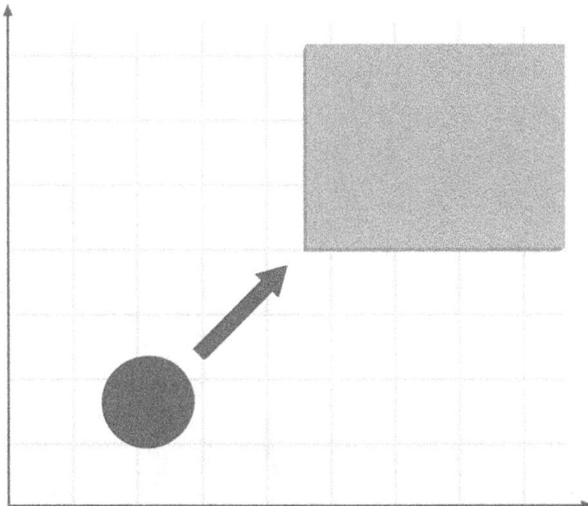

Here we have a scenario where the interviewer does not consider this strength as a key requirement in their hiring decision, and you have not identified this strength as one of your stronger strengths. This is an area you do not really want to be spending time on in an interview.

If you feel too much time is being spent on a discussion of this strength, lead the discussion back toward your positioning as smoothly and quickly as possible.

c) Undervalued Strength

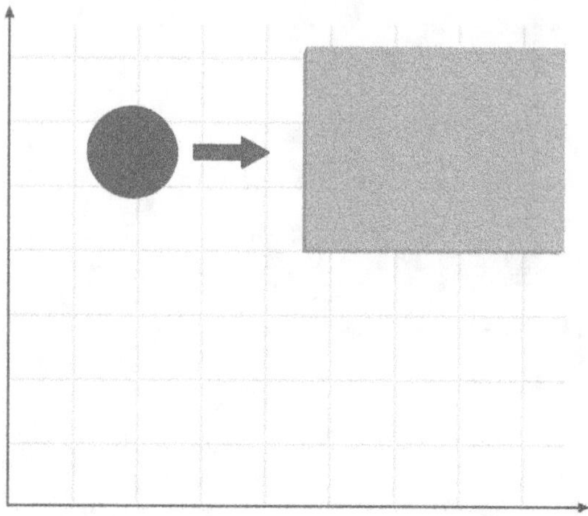

If you really believe this strength is *your* positioning, and the company is undervaluing this particular trait, then you have to first *sell* the interviewer on its importance. How can you do this? Give the interviewer a scenario that might happen in the future (or may be in now, based on your research!), where this strength is going to be key for the person in the role they are trying to fill. Find examples of similar companies using this strength and playing a key role in the company's success. Use stories from your past experiences, and relate them to the business of the targeted company. Explain how you utilized this strength to help your current/former company. This latter strategy works well because it also moves the strength to the forefront (more important on the scale) and, at the same time, gives an example from your past experience that allows you to claim ownership of this ladder.

Personal Story: I was once responsible for the launch of a pharmaceutical product that was fourth in its product class (ladder). Being fourth down a product ladder can be the "kiss of death" for any product. We knew simply claiming it was "in a successful product class" and "it worked" was not going to make it the market leader. So we created a new ladder (better to be number one on a new ladder than number four on the current one!). This new ladder was based on a very specific characteristic of the product, one that none of the other products had demonstrated. This feature of the product had a benefit for a specific sub-group of patients. But, at this point, physicians did not look for this characteristic in their patients, and so they thought our benefit was not important.

We first set out to educate healthcare professionals, based on evidence, about why they should look for this specific characteristic in their patients. Once this was accepted and patients were identified, we explained how our product could help these patients. We had "created" a new ladder; we increased the importance of the ladder in our customers' minds and then claimed the ladder as ours with the clinical evidence for our product. While we knew there would be a significant population of patients who would benefit from our product, the new ladder actually grew in greater importance and size than even we had expected and, as our product owned the top of the ladder, the product actually did became the number one product in its category.

d) Their Need is Not Your Biggest Strength

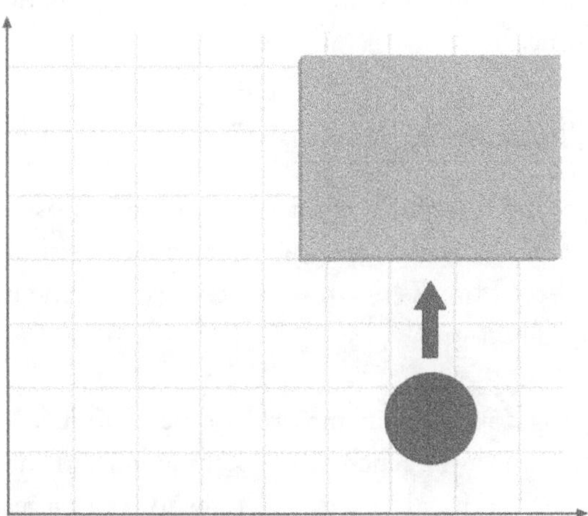

The company has a clear need for a specific strength. You do not feel this is your strongest strength based on the examples you can describe. You are also aware other candidates may be stronger in this area. You can consider two things. 1) Do you have a better story from your past demonstrating this behaviour favourably? Ask your friends, former colleagues, and mentors to help you, or, 2) If this strength is key to being hired into your target position, how can you make this strength stronger / ranked higher? This could involve volunteering for a not-for-profit organization or setting up your own project to make something happen.

Back to our earlier example

In our example, at the start of this section, with abilities to *juggle priorities* and *public speaking*. What would you choose or do?

Given only these two choices, you might either: a) work within the interview to strengthen the importance of *juggling priorities* and give examples of where you have used this strength to the benefit of your company, or b) get out and do some *public speaking*, perhaps on a specialized topic within your industry and talk about this endeavor in your interview. You might consider joining an organization such as *Toastmasters* or to taking a course on public speaking to strengthen your resume.

Your own personal "Positioning Statement"

Once you have carefully thought this through and have chosen your positioning, it is time to write your own "Personal Positioning Statement". Worksheet J breaks down your personal statement into easy straight forward sections.

By section:

"To": Write the hiring company's name or the type of industry in which you are looking for a job, such as, "**To** companies in the earth moving business." It is critical to state exactly who your target employer is. It gives you focus and ensures you do not lose sight of who you are selling yourself to.

"I": Write your name.

". . . am <u>the</u> candidate for the position of . . .": Note, "**<u>the</u>**" in Worksheet J is bolded and underlined for a specific reason. *You* have to *believe* you are the best candidate before, during, and after the interview. You have to believe you are the best prepared and the best presented, if you are going to sell yourself successfully. Believe in all the work you have put in, believe they are looking for you!

". . . who is most likely to succeed, because I offer the company someone who . . .": This is where your key strength / positioning goes. What are you offering that makes you the ideal candidate for this position?

". . . and I can support this from my experience by discussing . . .": Write out the stories you can use to illustrate your positioning and why the company needs these strengths..

This may / will take a few tries, so use pencil or photocopy the page a few times first. You will need to work on it, and after the next section of this chapter, you will see why.

You can find some examples of personal positioning statements in Appendix 2.

Worksheet J

Your Personal Positioning Statement

"To..,
(hiring company's name)

I, ..., am **the** candidate for
(my name / Brand)

the position of..,

who is most likely to succeed, because I offer the

company someone who ....

....,

and I can support this from my experience by

discussing ....

....

...."

The positioning statement is the most important thing about any brand – especially when the brand is you! Therefore, choosing your positioning will be one of the hardest things you ever do. It is so important that once you think you have it right, go out and do your own market research to see if it makes sense to anyone else!

Testing the Message

Have you ever been accosted in the street by a man or woman with a clipboard and pen in hand asking you if you have time to help with some market research, perhaps in exchange for a cup of tea or glass of orange juice and a cookie? I have. I always agree to answer their questions. In fact, much to the dismay of my family, I will cross the road every time to complete a survey because I am curious to find out what marketing challenge they are trying to address!

Personal Story: The market research that first made me think about this positioning concept took place a number of years back. I was walking down a busy city street when I was approached. A group of 7-10 young men were asked to watch a series of five TV commercials. The products varied, but I remember that one, in the middle, focused on the various features and benefits (strengths) of a new car. After watching all the commercials, we were asked to list which commercials we remembered watching, and then what we specifically remembered about the car commercial. After that, we were asked even more specific questions, such as, whether we remembered how quickly the car accelerated from zero to sixty. Then, we were given our drink and a cookie and sent on our way.

What did I learn from this experience? The key, was the researchers were measuring what *I heard* the company say about their product in their ad, rather than what *they said* to me in the commercial. Put another way, in this case, they wanted me to remember the car's acceleration and would only be happy if I could repeat this information back to them. That I had heard, understood and remembered this information was critical to the commercial's success. I was their target audience, and they wanted to make sure everyone in my group, had remembered what was obviously their positioning message.

If we had not remembered this key message from the commercial, then the researchers would have gone away and had the company change how they delivered the message and retested the commercial again with another target group until they consistently heard groups repeat the correct positioning message back to them. Their goal was to ensure their commercial communicated clearly their product's positioning and that they owned the top rung of a very specific ladder in our minds.

There have been some great creative commercial campaigns – many have even won numerous creative advertising awards. However for many of these award winning ads, the product owners have ultimately pulled the advertisements because the commercials, while creatively being superb, did not actually *sell* more of the brand! In these cases, the TV audience was entertained by the commercial but failed to remember the brand's key message.

With this story and your positioning statement in mind, what should you do now?

a) Just go for it in the next interview and trust your instincts, OR

b) Test it with some friends.

My "OR" was the big clue!

Testing your Message

Do what the car company did in the example above. You think you know what your positioning statement says, but how do people interpret it for themselves when they hear it?

Invite three to five friends over for drinks. After a little while, tell them you have something you want to try with them, a little game. Tell them five things, perhaps some trivia about the local area or other friends. Somewhere in the middle of this trivia state your positioning. Then, ask them not to discuss what you have said and change the conversation to some other topic of mutual interest. After an hour or so ask them each to write down the statement you made about yourself.

How close did they get? What words did they use? Discuss with each of them what they wrote down, particularly if the answer was not quite what you had said. What did they misunderstand? If there is a common misunderstanding, work on your wording again, and try it out another evening with a different group of people.

You can also tell them the stories you plan to use to support your positioning. Ask them if these stories actually support your positioning in their minds.

If you can find a group of friends in a similar or related industry as the one you are entering that would be ideal, particularly if your positioning includes some common language for that specific industry.

How to tell the story

There are many ways that positioning can be communicated, and, frankly, no one will care which one you use – as long as the message is interesting, you are confident, engaging, and you stay relevant to the listener.

The classic style is the "elevator pitch," or the "30 second commercial."

The idea of the elevator pitch is to imagine that you find yourself in an elevator with a potential employer. The average ride on an elevator is usually no more than 30 seconds, so, in that time, you must present why your potential employer should hire you before the doors open. This concept is also a classic training ground for entrepreneurs who are faced with a potential investor in the elevator, and they have 30 seconds to pitch why the investor should invest in their company. This timeframe also fits with radio and TV commercials. Too much longer, and your audience begins to disengage.

Framing the positioning as a question to grab the interviewer's attention and immediately engage them in your story can also be very effective.

"Have you ever been in a situation where you just cannot figure out why the financial numbers don't add up?" [Pause] "The people I have worked for have come to rely on me as the person they turn to, to find the answer!"

Whenever possible, it is advantageous to use stories to communicate messages.

Again, there is no right or wrong way for a message to be communicated, as long as:

a) You are confident,

b) It comes across as natural, not rehearsed (which means you have to rehearse a lot!), and

c) You have tested the wording of the message to ensure the positioning is heard and interpreted as you intended it.

Chapter Takeaways:

- Your own product positioning will take some time to develop.
- The rankings and ratings will guide you to consider different alternatives.
- You can choose only one ladder.
- Test out your positioning.
- What you say is important, but not as important as knowing what your target audience actually hears you say, and what they remember.

Next Steps

In the next chapter we will explore how to use your knowledge, experience and personal positioning statement to promote yourself.

NOTES

Chapter 8

BRINGING IT ALL TOGETHER THE COMMUNICATION PLAN

ALL OF YOUR WORKSHEETS SHOULD now have been completed, your positioning statement has been developed, tested and finalized, and your stories have been practiced. You are ready for the interview. Now it is all a matter of clear communication.

The importance of the method and style of your communication runs throughout the whole interview process, including:

- Cover Letter and Resume

When someone reads your resume, what stands out? Not sure? Then test it. Just as with your positioning statement, give your resume to 5 or 6 people (in this case, preferably strangers) and ask each of them to write down the ONE key thing they take from the resume which they believe to be the key strength you are trying to communicate. When you have their answers back ask them for their rationale, and what, if anything, they found distracting. If these answers do not match your desired message then go back and re-draft another version to test. There are many good books about writing resumes. Invest in one!

The same should now be done with the cover letter. For example, does it make your case for why you should be interviewed?

- The Interview

"You never get a second chance to make a first impression". It is *very* difficult to get the job offer when you make a poor initial impression with the interviewer – there are likely just too many other capable candidates.

Prepare, Prepare, Prepare.

How do you prepare for an interview? There is only one way: have all your information at hand and… "Practice! Practice! Practice!"… and practice out loud!

Think: wedding day, car race pit stop crews, professional sports teams.

Think: driving test, Broadway show, final exam.

Think: piano recital, circus performer, performance appraisal.

Everything in this list has two things in common. They are very important to the participants and people practice endlessly to get it right.

So why is it that when it comes to an interview we prepare for just a few questions (perhaps… if there is time) and then feel we can just wing it? Are we really that confident, or do we just feel embarrassed to dry run? Believe me, you will feel more embarrassed to fall short in the real interview than fluffing some answers while practicing for the interview!

How can you prepare?

Find ways to practice your answers out loud.

Speaking your answers in front of a mirror can help. Write your questions on cards and write your ideal answer on the back. If possible, find a real live person to ask the interview questions and give you feedback on how well they understood your answers. Did your answers give your crisp, clear positioning? You can check this by having them repeat back the answer as they recall you saying it. To really learn from the experience, and add a little real stress, use a camcorder or computer to record youself as you answer the questions. Watching the video can be sobering, and perhaps a little embarrassing. But, if you really want to know how others see you – complete with "ums", "ers" and "likes" – this is the way to learn.

Appendix 3 has some commonly used general interview questions you might want to consider. You should also think of more job-specific questions by again putting yourself in the interviewer's seat and thinking about what you would ask if you were the interviewer trying to identify the ideal candidate.

How do you feel?

Your "frame of mind" is also very important when you go into the interview. You want to visualize doing a great job in the interview. Be positive that you are ready for any question and believe that *you are* the person receiving a job offer.

In addition to your enthusiasm, when you go into an interview, keep two things in mind....

1. I want to show myself in the best possible light and successfully present my positioning,

2. I want to ensure the person interviewing me is the kind of person I want to work for and represents a company I can feel passionate about.

Personal Story: I once went to a second and final interview for a position I really wanted. I was apparently an odds-on favorite with the recruiting agency and an industrial psychologist who had previously interviewed and tested me. However, I went to the interview with a black tie in my pocket. After my interview, I was going to attend a funeral for someone I was close to. Do you think I put on my best show in the interview, knowing I was going to a funeral afterward? No way, and I could feel it. No enthusiasm and importantly, no connection with my interviewer. My emotions were very different than the ones I needed, and, to make matters worse, the interviewer was jet-lagged, and there was no way my enthusiasm was going to carry him through to a good interview. Not surprisingly, I did not get the job. I do not blame the interviewer – this interview was a one-shot deal and I flunked. In retrospect, I should have asked for the interview to be moved to a different day, or, at the very least, ensured the potential employer understood what was happening. Would I have gotten the job? I don't know, but I certainly was not ready to sell myself well in the scenario I put myself in.

■ Interview follow up

After the interview, I always recommended you follow up with a short letter (not electronic) of thanks for their consideration. Amid these "pleasantries", do not forget to remind your interviewer of your positioning and how you will add the value they are looking for. Write why you want the role, re-state what you can offer, and thank them for their time. Remind them of your key strength, how you have shown this strength in the past, and how it will benefit their company in the future. If you have gone through a recruitment agency, see what they have learned about how your interview went and use that additional intelligence to craft your follow up letter. Each follow up letter should be unique to the position you have interviewed for – do not create a standard form letter! People can get jobs based on this seeming courtesy; this reminder of you and your positioning can set you apart from the other applicants. One last word on follow up letters... always have someone you trust read them over for spelling, punctuation and grammatical errors.... every contact leaves an impression about you.

■ Your References

All too often, candidates do a lot of good work in the interview only to be foiled by their *referees* or *references,* people chosen by the candidate to vouch for them. Don't leave any stone unturned, especially this one. This is your career. Ask your references to share what they are going to say about you. Do their answers support your positioning? If not, why not? Your positioning is probably what led the employer to interview you and seek out and talk to your references, so why would you want your references to say anything else? Pick references who identify with your personal positioning, so much so that they can easily give their own examples to support your positioning.

Personal Story: When someone asks me to be one of their references, I always ask for a copy of their resume and ask what they would like me to highlight (their positioning). Note that I do not ask them what they want me to say, but what their key message is. If I do not agree with the key message, I let them know *before* they give my name to the potential employer.

You should be concerned about what the references will say, so why not do a dry run over the phone? Ask them to answer the questions they will probably be asked, based on the position you are going for. See Appendix 4 for some general "dry run" questions to use. Remember, your references will already have a positioning for you in their mind and this may be different than the positioning you have crafted for yourself. They have had experience with you, seen you at work, and seen you under pressure. All these circumstances may have given them a different impression than what you believe them to have. Help them understand your positioning and ask what personal examples they might give to support that positioning. If they do not feel they can support your stated positioning, move on and find other references who can. It is your future after all.

Chapter Takeaways:

- Everything you do should reflect your positioning
- Practice! Practice! Practice out loud!
- Rehearse with your references

Next Step

You now have everything you need to make a good impression in the interview, and you are well rehearsed in your positioning and stories. In the next chapter I will touch on one more element that you may consider to really stand out as a candidate. "Going the extra mile" suggests there is still plenty of room for some innovation in how you present yourself to the hiring company.

NOTES

Chapter 9

GOING THE EXTRA MILE

THERE ARE SOME BASICS YOU must have to get a job offer. These may be considered "admission tickets" - if you do not have these there is no way you will ever be even considered for a second interview, let alone a job offer. "Admission tickets" may include basic things such as: showing up on time for the interview, demonstrating at least a basic knowledge of the company's business, products or services, and competitors, and being able to express interest and enthusiasm for the position during the interview process.

Then there is what I think of as "going the extra mile" points.

"Going the extra mile", to me, consists of having the ability to demonstrate, in an interview, that you have really invested time prior to the meeting, in order to understand the interviewing company's business, products or services. You can demonstrate you have not only invested time gaining *knowledge* (note: not just *data* and *information* – a key distinction), but you have also invested time in considering, and strategizing around what the company might be facing, and perhaps what role you might play in helping the company achieve its desired goals.

I can not tell you exactly what "going the extra mile" will look like to every interviewer, in every hiring situation (remembering that there are specific "admission ticket" items for specific jobs), however, I can suggest you think about what you *need to know*, and what would be *impressive* for you to consider and know. Just think, perhaps the strengths you demonstrate in "going the extra mile" may even be strengths the hiring company is looking for: understanding the business, or, ability to strategize, or, ability to communicate a business situation and offer solutions etc.

Personal Story I: It's funny, but when I was younger, I was a lot less aware of what people's expectation of me might be... I just did what I thought was right to do in order to achieve a goal. Fresh out of university, I wanted to use my degree (biological chemistry) in pursuing a job and had heard that a life science degree was an "admission ticket" for becoming a pharmaceutical sales representative. I had a number of interviews with different companies and I had not got even a whiff of a job offer. About the fifth headhunter I met was an older lady in a big, old city office. All I remember, is at the end of our meeting, she put down her cigarette (it was some time ago!), looked me straight in the eyes, and told me that companies probably thought I looked too young to be credible selling the advantages and disadvantages of pharmaceutical products to doctors. She told me, bluntly, if I wanted to get a pharmaceutical sales representative job I had to go out and at least get some sales experience - it didn't matter in what field. I immediately went out and got a sales position in one of the toughest, most competitive jobs... selling insurance. Within two weeks of going through my insurance sales training, I had two interviews with two different major pharmaceutical companies. During the interviews, I told them I was selling insurance and why I had taken on this job. Both companies offered me a job after a first interview! I do not think they offered me a job because I was now an experienced salesman, or that insurance sales had somehow aged me. I know, because I asked after they offered the jobs, the main reason they wanted me to work for them was because I was prepared to "go the extra mile". I had been told I needed to prove I wanted to sell and I was prepared to do what it took to achieve my goal. I tangibly demonstrated a behavior, or rather, a competency, both companies were looking for in their job applicants.

Personal Story 2: One of those two interviews I had in the last story was with a really well respected, industry leading company. They had called me at noon one day and they asked me to interview the next day, their last day of interviewing for a vacant sales territory. I had less than 24 hours, but I decided I should find out as much as possible about them. So, I went to my family physician's office, and got permission from the receptionist to sit in the waiting room until the next pharmaceutical sales representative came in. The next representative who walked in was willing to talk to me. He answered all my questions, including, what he thought of the company I was having the interview with. I then went to the local pharmacy and asked the pharmacist to tell me about the company's products. She did this, and, as an added bonus, told me about the newest product they were discussing with healthcare professionals. I did not have time to memorize all of the company's products I had written down, so I took it to the interview, and sheepishly took it out and read from it when I was asked what I knew about the company. I felt a little embarrassed. They asked why and how I came to have the list. I told them and a little to my surprise they still offered me the job. I did accept the job, and a few months later I asked my new boss why they were so confident in offering me the job on the spot. He told me it was because I had again "gone the extra mile" with both selling insurance and creating my product list. With regards to my product list, it was not the information I had that was so important, it was rather with less than 24 hours to the interview I had cared enough and wanted the job enough, to go out and seek the information from credible sources. As it turned out this is a good competency for a sales representative to have.

Personal Story 3: Of all the people I have interviewed over the years, especially for more senior roles, I have to say very few have "gone the extra mile". Those who do invariably get the job and are always surprised when I tell them why. They always say exactly what I said to my boss after he told me why he had offered me a pharmaceutical sales position: "but doesn't everyone do that?"

No they don't, but they should!

Companies can also do research on you!

A word of caution is in order here. Employers can now do a lot more research on you than just looking at your resume and talking to your references. The same on-line and networking sources you use to research the company can also be used by the company to research you.

To be really future-proofed, it's worth researching yourself to find out what potential employers may be able to find out about you. What is your public profile? What do you look like as a potential employee to someone who does not know you? Think about future employers looking at you on LinkedIn, FaceBook, Friends Reunited, Bebo, Twitter, MySpace, and other social networking sites. Do your own research, or perhaps ask someone else you trust to research you. What do they come up with? Does it match your resume and your positioning?

What else can *you* do?

Don't just sit back and hope you are already the best candidate. It is never too late to build on your strengths, or to add to your skills and resume.

If you look at your worksheets and decide you need new or more recent examples of your strengths to discuss with the interviewer (always a good idea), or you want to ensure you fly past the benchmark level for "admission ticket" items, go out and *make* them happen. What have you got to lose, except the job you really want?

Here are just a few examples of what you might do.

Volunteering:

Many non-profit groups and associations are looking for resources to help in professional areas as well as to create a wider network with the profit sector. Doing work here, even part-time, can work on many levels; 1) you can learn new, or build on particular strengths, and 2) many companies today want to be more involved with their communities through non-profit organizations and will likely appreciate your contacts and ideas.

Volunteering gives you the chance to demonstrate skills or competencies your previous jobs might not have encouraged. Become a treasurer, a secretary, a team leader, an action-oriented go-getter, or a fund raiser who goes door-to-door or out looking for corporate donors. Talking to different companies in your chosen industry about your community work is also a great way to set up a network and meet new connections in a company you would like to join. Taking on any of these roles enables you to support your current strengths or perhaps find ones you didn't know you had. And, if it is for a good cause, you will feel good about the time you are investing.

Mentoring:

If you have been in an industry for a number of years, look for any opportunity to mentor people. It is an opportunity to expand your people and communication skills, as well as your network. The ability to deal with people is usually one of the most important aspects of any job. Think back: other people probably mentored you, so it's also a good way to give back and help someone else get a break. Doing good, I believe, begets something good happening to you.

Back to school:

"Always willing to learn" is a good competency to demonstrate in a fast changing marketplace. I always tell people I meet that each year I would expect them to have learned something valuable enough to add to and strengthen their resume. Look at your *strength* list and compare it to the *needs* section from your potential employer. Is something missing from your list? If you can identify a gap can you also identify how you might fill this gap? Are there appropriate courses available? Full-time, weekend, evenings? It may take some money and a whole lot of commitment, but missing a job you want because of a missing skill is a shame. Taking a course that helps you better meet the requirements of the potential new employer also shows your commitment and determination when you set your mind to something.

Personal Story: After some time as a medical representative, I decided I wanted a pharmaceutical marketing job at head office. So, I followed the advice of a friend of mine who worked in marketing. This friend had completed a *Diploma in Marketing* prior to getting her marketing job. This, I figured, would make me much more attractive for the marketing job I wanted, compared to the other interested pharmaceutical medical representatives around me. I studied and completed the diploma at nights at a local collage, and not long after completing the course I interviewed and was offered the marketing job I wanted in head office.

While I was in my first year in marketing, it was suggested I might want to take an *Accounting and Finance* course to get ahead in business. I did, and, based on my willingness to manage my job and the course at the same time, I got significant credit and consideration for a more senior role.

If you can show continued professional and/or personal growth, the people interviewing you will see you have made an investment to improve yourself and make yourself more valuable. This investment shows an ongoing commitment in yourself and your personal brand.

Most jobs are found through networking

It is a reality that you will not get the opportunity to interview for all the job openings that are ideally suited for you. In the majority of cases positions are filled either by internal candidates or through a company's external "network". It is therefore good practice for you to take every chance you get to become part of the informal network by interacting with potential employers or employment influencers (someone who might be able to recommend you for an interview: For example, current employees, suppliers, search consultants) and telling them your positioning.

Another objective for your job search is to get into these informal networks.

Here are a few ways to increase your network reach:

Take a deep breath, and;

- go to industry association meetings, and actively work the room... introduce yourself to people and tell them your positioning,
- volunteer to work for an association,
- volunteer to present at industry meetings, leaving them with a message about you and your positioning,
- do some consulting work for prospective employers, ideally utilizing your positioning,
- write an article for a newspaper or industry newsletter or write an informative blog or "white paper" and put it on-line.

Why did I say just before this list, "..., take a deep breath..."?

Because these are the sort of things that everyone says they will do, but most people put off doing – believing, at some level, it is beyond them or that the opportunity would never exist for them. Well believe me, these opportunities are plentiful if you just go out and ask – and if these things are in a strength area of yours, then you can excel. You just have to take that deep breath and jump in!

In all these activities you are making connections and sharing. By casting your net in these different ways, you will find that not everyone has your strengths and in fact your strengths are in demand.

But these things don't just happen – you have to let other people know what you are good at, and that is what these activities do.

Chapter Takeaways:

- How can you "Go the Extra Mile"?
- Always look to improve your resume through ongoing formal or informal learning.
- Increase your networking… most jobs don't appear in the classified section.
- You, and only you are responsible for your Positioning.

NOTES

Chapter 10

FINAL THOUGHTS

WHERE DID WE START AT the beginning of this book? We talked about reality TV, and we considered how this relates to today's standard interview process… one is as crazy as the other! We learned that interviewing, while it is not an ideal process, is the process in which we must learn to excel.

If you have completed each step of this book, I hope you have not only learned something about marketing and selling, and the interview process, but also learned something very positive about yourself.

I trust you now understand what your strengths are, and perhaps, what you really want to do as a career, and always follow with passion.

You have learned:

- not everyone is the same; everyone brings a different set of skills and competencies to the table,
- everyone looks at life through different frames,
- you have a great deal to offer an employer and this should be made very clear through all your communications,
- you have to do your homework, and be prepared to "go the extra mile",

- positioning is the core of marketing and sales, and you should consider yourself a brand and know how to promote yourself.

And finally, you have learned that:

- you, and only you, are responsible for your positioning and making things happen!

If you would like to read a little more, get copies of some worksheets or send me feedback on what has worked for you, please go to:

www.nowpickme.com.

Appendix I

SOME EXAMPLE COMPETENCIES

Action Orientated

Just gets things done – makes a step by step plan for moving forward and then moves quickly to get the steps completed.

Deals with Ambiguity

Able to deal with change and make a decision even when some information is missing.

Customer Focus

Is continually focused on identifying means of meeting and exceeding customer expectations.

Conflict Management

Is not afraid of facing conflict head on in order to find a resolution and move forward.

Creative

Identifies challenges, understands its dynamics and can come up with innovative alternatives.

Timely Decision Making

Makes tough decisions under pressure or stress.

Ethics and Values

Has an appropriate set of values for any situation and acts in line with these values.

Hiring and Staffing

Builds a strong team through identification and hiring of strong performers.

Building Team Spirit

Within team or company builds a positive spirit or moral even in stressful times.

Priority Setting

Quickly focus on what is most important and gets it done.

Managerial Courage

Says it like it is – lets everyone know what the situation is and directs actions to move forward.

Managing and Measuring

Clearly sets out measurable expectations and milestones and puts in place methods to measure progress.

Negotiation

Finds win-win scenarios with internal or external customers and builds trust.

Organizing

Is able to co-ordinate multiple activities in order to complete all tasks within timelines.

Political Savvy

Identifies what is important to different individuals and groups and effectively avoids breakdowns in relationships.

Presentation Skills

Persuasively presents and sells complex ideas to groups of people.

Problem Solving

Has the ability to identify questions to understand a situation and then to identify the best solution.

Technical Learning

Is able to learn, understand and utilize technical information and data.

Appendix 2

EXAMPLES OF POSITIONING STATEMENTS

"TO THE MARKETING DIRECTOR OF company X , I, (name), am **the** candidate for the position of Product Manager, who is most likely to succeed, because I offer the company someone who can revitalize enthusiasm around a core brand. In support, I successfully re-energized a similar brand for my previous employer from a position of losing market share to one of recapturing market leadership."

"To the Sales Director of a major department store, I, (name), am **the** candidate for the position of Floor Manager, who is most likely to succeed, because I offer the company someone who finds innovative ways to increase sales. In support, I increased sales 23% for my current employer through a unique incentive program for my sales staff."

"To the President of the multi-national corporation, I, (name), am **the** candidate for the position of Personal Assistant, who is most likely to succeed, because I offer the company someone who can effectively multi-task to keep my boss organized and ahead of the game. In support, I coordinated the schedules for two senior executives who were each out of the office 70% of the time and never missed a meeting."

"To the Director of Finance, I, (name), am **the** candidate for the position of Account Receivable Representative, who is most likely to succeed, because I offer the company someone who is able to get the money owed by communicating effectively with customers on sometimes sensitive matters without them becoming upset with our company. In support, I improved the account receivables at my last company by 30% over an 8 month period."

"To the HR Director, I, (name), am **the** candidate for the position of Senior Recruiter, who is most likely to succeed, because I offer the company someone who has the flexibility to work with managers from all department in order to identify what they are really looking for in their job openings. In support, improvement of 10% in success rating of new hires, across all departments, at my prior company over each of the 3 years I was in my HR role."

NOTES

Appendix 3

COMMON QUESTIONS YOU MAY BE ASKED AND SHOULD BE PREPARED FOR!

- Tell me about yourself.
- What do you know about our company / industry?
- Describe a team you have worked on in the past that had a difficult task;
  - what role did you play on the team?
  - what was the outcome for the team, and how did you influence this result?
- Describe a time when you had to deal with a difficult customer
  - what did you do?
  - what was the outcome?
- Describe a time when you had a conflict with someone in your organization
  - what did you do?
  - what was the outcome?
- Why did you leave your last position?
- What are your long term goals for the future (3 years, 5 years, 10 years)?

- How would others describe you? Boss / Peer / Subordinate / Customer?
    - why? can you describe a time when you think you exemplified this trait?
- What do you think you offer this company?
- What accomplishment are you most proud of?
    - why?
    - what did you do specifically?
- What weaknesses do you have?
- What do you think your priorities will be coming into this job?
- Describe your ideal working environment.
- Describe a difficult boss you have had in the past.
    - how did you deal with them?
- Describe a time when you were faced with something new.
    - what did you do?
    - what was the outcome?

Pick any competency from Appendix I that you believe to be important to the employee and ask:

- do you consider yourself to be (insert competency)?
- describe a situation that you believe best exemplifies you strength with (insert competency).

Appendix 4

SAMPLE QUESTIONS FOR YOUR REFERENCES

REFERENCE... WHEN ASKED THE FOLLOWING, how would you respond:

- How do you know the candidate?
- If you worked with the candidate – over what period of time?
- What do you consider are the candidates key strengths?
  - what makes you say this? Can you give examples?
- What are the candidates weaknesses?
  - what makes you say this? Can you give examples?
- Can you describe a time when you saw the candidate under pressure – how did they respond to this pressure?
- Can you describe a time when the candidate had to work in a team.
  - what role did the candidate play?
  - what was the outcome for the team, and how do you think the candidate contributed to this outcome?

NOTES

NOTES

NOTES

NOTES

www.ingramcontent.com/pod-product-compliance
Lightning Source LLC
Chambersburg PA
CBHW051547170526
45165CB00002B/921